Old BUSBY

by

Busby History Group and Maud Devine

Bonnyton cottages formed a hamlet or fermtoun situated on the right of way between Newford Grove and the River Cart. The settlement was originally known as Bonnyhouse. Although the cottages were demolished about a century ago, the name is perpetuated by Bonnyton House, a nearby home for the elderly.

© Busby History Group and Maud Devine 2003
First published in the United Kingdom, 2003,
by Stenlake Publishing
Telephone / Fax: 01290 551122
Printed by Cordfall Ltd, Glasgow, G21 2QA

ISBN 1 84033 281 8

The publishers regret that they cannot supply copies of any pictures featured in this book.
Copies of those pictures provided by East Renfrewshire Council (see acknowledgements), may be obtained by contacting Giffnock Library.

ACKNOWLEDGEMENTS

Busby History Group would like to thank the community for its generosity in contributing photographs, knowledge and memories to this book, as well as East Renfrewshire Cultural Services for support, professional advice and contributions from its photographic archive. Particular thanks are due to Liz English, Chairwoman of Busby History Group, for her tireless enthusiasm in collecting material for the project. Special mention must also be made of the late Ian Craig ARPS, a skilled photographer and indefatigable collector and preserver of the history of Busby in all its forms, as well as David Anderson, also a photographer of Busby past and present. Thanks also to W. Gordon Carslaw, Maris Craig, Margaret Denholm, Helen English, Jean Hume (née Fraser), Sheila Innes (née Turner), Ken Melvin, Stuart Nisbet, Elsie Robbie (née McFarlane) and Mary Young. The group would like to acknowledge the contributions of Charlie Frame, Bobby Gorman, Jimmy Thomson and Willie Woodward who are, sadly, now deceased.

In addition to those listed above, Stenlake Publishing would like to thank Maud Devine for co-ordinating this project, W. A. C. Smith for providing the pictures on pages 27, 28 and 29, and East Renfrewshire Council for providing the pictures on pages 1, 4, 9, 10 (upper), 11–17, 19, 26, 32–34, 38 (upper) and 44.

BUSBY HISTORY GROUP

Busby History Group was founded to collect, preserve and make available the history of Busby as a place and community. Its members are: Ann Andrews, Charles Bryan, Liz English, Ann Ferguson, Bill Ferguson, Isobel Kitson, Pamela Long and Lilias Mackay.

FURTHER READING

The books listed below were used by the authors during their research. None of them are available from Stenlake Publishing. Those interested in finding out more are advised to contact their local bookshop or reference library.

Anderson, David, *A Family History of Busby*, 2000

Eastwood District Libraries, *Calico, Cotton and Character – A History of Busby*, 1988

History of Busby District School, 1876–1976

Looking Down the Years, Busby West Parish Church 1835–1985

McBeath, H. D., *Walks by Busby and Thorntonhall with Historical Notes on the Area*, 1980

Nisbet, Stuart, Busby Cotton Mill, *Scottish Archaeology Gazette* No. 19, 1989

Nisbet, Stuart, Busby and Dovecothall Cotton Mills, *Renfrewshire Local History Forum Journal*, Vol. 2, 1990

Nisbet, Stuart, Newmill (Busby) – An Early Scottish Cotton Mill, *Scottish Industrial History* Vols. 11–13, 1990

Ross, Revd William, *Busby and its Neighbourhood*, 1883

Welsh, Dr Thomas, *Eastwood District, History & Heritage*

INTRODUCTION

Busby was originally called Bushby, meaning a bushy place, and the earliest known reference occurs in the name Adam de Bushbie in 1342. The lands of Busby were originally part of the Barony of Carmunnock and were situated wholly on the Lanarkshire (east) side of the White Cart Water. The earliest indications of habitation in Busby emanate from Busby Glen, where a bronze axe was found and an early hill fort survives.

It was the quality of water and motive power available from the White Cart Water which brought industry to Busby, and by the late 1770s a number of mills had been established along its banks. Working downstream from Waterfoot to Busby on the Lanarkshire bank of the Cart were Dripps waulk mill, Busby meal mill and Parker's waulk mill. On the Renfrewshire bank, between Waterfoot and Newmill, were Mearns or Letham meal mill, Dripps meal mill, Gateside lint mill, and Newmill meal and lint mills. The lint mills prepared or 'scutched' locally grown flax for spinning, while the waulk or fulling mills washed and thickened cloth.

In 1778 the lint and meal mills at Newmill were demolished, and what was only the third cotton spinning mill in Scotland was built by Glasgow merchant William Ferguson. It was called Newmill or Busby Upper Mill. A second cotton mill, Busby Lower Mill, was built further down the lade by James Doxon in 1790. Conditions were hard at the mills with a working week of at least twelve hours a day, six days a week in a hot, damp atmosphere where diseases such as bronchitis, pneumonia and tuberculosis were rife. Having changed ownership several times, the mills passed to James Crum in 1843, 'a remarkably able, accomplished and public spirited man who did a great deal for the village' (*Busby and its Neighbourhood*). In the 1780s Busby bridge was built across the Cart and thereafter the name Newmill faded away, with the land on both sides of the river being known as Busby.

Another major local business, the Busby printworks, was established in 1796 on the site of Busby meal mill. In 1829 the then owners, McKean & Peacock, provided a circulating library for their employees. Perhaps the most successful proprietors of the printworks were Inglis & Wakefield Ltd who ran them from 1842 and produced very high quality products, including printed calico. By 1883 the printworks covered 'an area of 7 acres, producing 3,000 pieces of printed goods daily and employing 600 workers' (T. E. Niven, *East Kilbride – the History of Parish and Village*). They were taken over by the Calico Printers Association in 1900 and closed in 1901. In the latter part of the twentieth century the area's industrial tradition was revived with the establishment of the White Cart industrial area.

Busby enjoyed its industrial peak during the second half of the nineteenth century, with its population rising from 902 in 1841 to 2,155 in 1881. By the end of the century, however, the fortunes of the Busby mills had waned, although the Lower Mill was used by the Busby Bleaching & Beetling Co. from 1888 until 1942. Today eighteen businesses are based on its site, fourteen of which are located within the former mill building.

A very important factor in the village's development was the building of the railway line from Pollokshaws to Busby (later extended to East Kilbride), carried out under the auspices of the Busby Railway Company. Busby station opened on 1 January 1866 and not only aided industry but contributed to the village's growth by making commuting to Glasgow possible. In 1904 the *Pollokshaws News* recommended the clean air of Busby to people with lung complaints.

The Glasgow architect Alexander 'Greek' Thomson extended Busby House in Field Road for Durham Kippen, the bleachworks' owner, in 1856. This should not be confused with the Crums' house, which was also called Busby House, and in 1897 became Dr Moore's Convalescent Home for Nurses. Both buildings were demolished in the 1960s to make way for flats.

During its nineteenth century heyday, Busby had a thriving social life with a literary society, Mechanics' Institute, library, one of Scotland's earliest penny savings banks, a small school, Overlee Cricket Club, Busby Bowling Club and Cartvale Football Club. Busby District School (now Busby Primary School) was opened in 1876.

In 1921 the Duff family made an important contribution to the village when they presented it with the Duff Memorial Hall in memory of their sons, Lieut. John Mitchell Duff and Lieut. William Duff, both of whom were killed in the First World War. Mr Duff, who died in 1934, was session clerk at Busby West Parish Church for 36 years. The hall complex was acquired by the council in 1959.

Busby West Parish Church opened on 8 May 1836. In 1865 a Free Church congregation was constituted and its church became Busby East Church. The Roman Catholic population which originally travelled to St Bridget's in Eaglesham had St Joseph's built in 1880 at the Sheddens with a school in its grounds. A new Catholic primary school was opened in Oliphant Crescent on 24 August 1964 and the church was rebuilt in 1971.

Many council houses were built in the 1950s and 60s, greatly increasing Busby's population. In 1968 the main part of the village was designated a Comprehensive Development Area, with provision made for housing for the elderly and new shops. The private housing boom helped encourage regeneration, and saw the building of smart streets and crescents in areas such as The Paddock. In spite of all these new developments Busby still retains its village character and the community has a strong sense of local identity.

It is at this point that Carmunnock Road (right) meets East Kilbride Road, and it was here, beside the station, that the original settlement of Busby started to grow on the eastern (Lanarkshire) side of the White Cart Water before the fifteenth century. On the right is the building that used to be Busby East Church, built to serve a Free Church congregation constituted in 1865. The Free Church was founded by the secession of 474 ministers (out of a total of 1,203) from the Church of Scotland on 18 May 1843 in a schism resulting from a conflict over the Established Church's acceptance of patronage, whereby congregations had no say in choosing their ministers. The rift was finally healed in 1929 when the Presbyterian Church joined with the United Free Church. In 1874 Busby East Church was greatly enlarged by the addition of the central portion of the building. Springbank, at 65 East Kilbride Road, was purchased as a manse in 1869. Nowadays the manse for Busby Parish Church is in Carmunnock Road. Busby East Church was burnt out in 1991 but its exterior was retained and the building has since been converted into flats.

This photograph of Eaglesham Road was taken in the early years of the twentieth century when only a few carts and horse buses used the road. The sign on the left reads 'Excellent sites for feuing. Moderate feu duties'. At the time Glasgow businessmen were beginning to move to areas within easy travelling distance of the city such as Busby, where they built elegant stone villas. Here Greenbank Church (also visible in the picture on page 39) is surrounded by open space, while today the main road has become completely built up and is busy with traffic.

Busby village in the early twentieth century, with children playing freely on a road devoid of traffic. The tenements furthest away from the camera on the left-hand side of the street are known as the Bank Buildings. They were built on the site of one of the five earliest houses on the Lanarkshire side of Busby village, and are shown on a plan dated 1787. Originally they were called the 'London Ring'. The name Bank Buildings may derive from any of the following sources: they are situated on the bank of the river; they were the location of the first Busby bank; one of the houses was owned by a Mr Bank.

Ian Craig's grocery was located in the Bank Buildings on East Kilbride Road. The Craig family have a long association with Busby, and Ian Craig, a skilled photographer and Associate of the Royal Photographic Society, was responsible for collecting many of the photographs in this book, as well as taking several of them. In 1907 John Craig, a partner in the firm A. & J. Craig, Grocers and Wine Merchants, gave evidence to a parliamentary session in the struggle between Renfrew County Council and Glasgow Corporation for control of Busby Water Company. He testified that: 'The supply of water from the Water Company to this district has never been satisfactory . . . Nearly all the people in the place, tied a cloth over the tap of our water pipes to prevent solid matter getting into the water which we were using for domestic purposes . . . this cloth was required to be changed daily . . . when it was perfectly filthy, covered with insects.'

The top of Main Street showing Bull Road (leading off to the right) in the days before Cartsbridge Road had been built. Bull Road acquired its name from Alexander Wilson's Black Bull Inn, and was where Wilson's Hall was located, a focal point for social activities in the village where dances and magic lantern shows were held and silent movies screened. On the left of the picture is 13 Main Street. Allan Gray recalls: 'Typical of the properties in the old village was No. 13, owned by my father in the early years of the century. These two-storey houses were entered through a 'pend' with outside toilets under the stairs and on the upper stair landing.' Mr Gray's joinery firm, Allan Gray & Son, was run from a large, timber two-storey building with electrically-powered, shaft-driven woodworking machinery on the ground floor. Miss Martha (Mattie) Gray, was for many years the registrar of births, deaths and marriages for the parish and operated from home for a considerable period before moving to an office in the Sheddens about the mid-1940s. Eventually all the houses except No. 13 were condemned as unfit and subsequently demolished.

Dating from the nineteenth century, this business was originally called the Cartvale Spirit Vaults. It later became Mac's Bar, changing its name to the Cartvale Public House in 1910 before becoming the Sutherland Arms and then reverting to the Cartvale. Beside the pub was a small shop owned by Miss Milly Frame. Milly and her brother Jock lived in a small house behind the pub. Two blocks up from the Cartvale stands the earliest surviving cottage in Main Street with its external stair at the front of the building. This used to be the home and workplace of Martha Gray, the registrar of births, deaths and marriages. There was a second inn in the village called the Black Bull, owned by Alexander Wilson. William Mann, County Councillor, who died in 1904, was a great temperance campaigner and chairman of the Malletsheugh Water and Drainage District. Through the Temperance Act the public houses in Mearns Parish were reduced to two in number at the start of the twentieth century. One was in Busby (the Cartvale) and the other at Malletsheugh just outside Mearns village. Today the Cartvale remains a focal and social point in the village.

A look through the valuation rolls for the Parish of Mearns in the late nineteenth century shows just how many shops and businesses there were in Busby's Main Street. These included Robert Paterson the tailor, whom Ian Craig of Busby remembers sitting cross-legged on the floor and making old-fashioned suits which could not be bought in the more modern shops of Glasgow. Also listed are Agnes Cunningham's wash-house; Walter Seal the engraver; George Paterson, bookseller; James Brown, draper; John Pollok, shoemaker; Campolini, ice-cream merchant; Busby Co-op; Archibald Lindsay's bakehouse; the Billiard Saloon; Findlay, the baker; MacFarlane's apothecary and Wilson's Inn (i.e. the Black Bull).

This photograph was taken at the rear of Durham Terrace and the style of dress suggests a date of the late 1930s. It is believed that the ladies may be members of the Irvine family. During the 1930s tenement dwellings began to lose favour amongst councils as many of them required major refurbishment (substantial numbers lacked bathrooms, for instance). Instead, emphasis was shifted to building terraced or semi-detached houses with gardens. Examples in Busby include the houses in Birch Crescent and Avenue, Cartsbridge Road and Elm Street, although the local housebuilding programme was interrupted by the Second World War. Tenements tended to have a wash-house in the back court with a rota drawn up amongst residents for its use. Whoever had the morning slot needed to get up early to light the fire beneath the boiler so that there was a supply of hot water for when the washing began. Clean clothes were wrung out using a mangle before being hung out to dry.

This view of Main Street probably dates from the 1950s as the Austin car outside Christine Marshall's shop is from that period. Opposite the Austin is the Equis' café and their ice cream van. The three-storey tenement at the left of the picture has since been demolished. Beside Miss Marshall's shop is the Duff Memorial Hall, built in 1921/22 by William Duff as a memorial to his sons, Lieutenants John and William Duff, both of whom were killed in the First World War. The halls included hot baths and a swimming pool (known locally as Bob's Puddle), a library, reading room and social room. Jean Hume (née Fraser) notes that the girls and boys got to use the baths on alternate days. At this time many of the houses in Busby had no baths of their own and had outside toilets. During the winter the swimming pool was covered over and the surface used for carpet bowls. Today the former baths complex houses Busby library and a set of halls used for many activities by Busby villagers.

Christine Marshall ran a general drapery in Busby for many years. There was a tenement block called Cartland, now demolished, adjacent to her shop. Gordon Carslaw remembers: 'my dad and his brother and two younger sisters were brought up in a ground floor room and kitchen [in this block] together with their parents'. Cartland also housed the old post office, which was run by the Thomsons and was combined with a hardware shop. Busby's population rose sharply from 1,921 in 1951 to 5,333 in 1961, and along with new council housing to keep up with this increase a new set of shops was built in Main Street, one of which houses the modern Busby post office.

Toni Equi took over the running of Equis' Café from his parents, Charlie and Marie Equi, in the late 1930s. The Equis were very popular and local people remember the café and chip shop as being immaculate. Toni used to sell huge boxes of chocolates in the run-up to Christmas and would raffle off any unsold ones afterwards. In later years the family ran a very successful café and restaurant at Charing Cross, Glasgow. The public toilet at the far right of the picture has now been demolished.

This view of Main Street shows the heart of the old village with the Cartvale Bar on the left and the Duff Memorial Hall on the right. A house was knocked down to make way for the Central Garage (with its Esso sign), a business which had disappeared by the early 1980s. Beside the pub was Milly Frame's 'jenny a' things' shop, so-called because of the wide range of goods it sold. This was subsequently taken over by Mrs Cuturi, an Irish lady who opened the shop seven days a week and sold newspapers on a Sunday. Mrs Johnson had a small shop opposite the end of Cartsbridge Road. She only sold toys and it is hard to imagine how she earned a living.

The land between Cartsbridge Road, Busby Road and Flesher's Park was known as the Plantation and was a favourite play area for Busby children. Around 1960, the flats and houses of Hill Crescent were built by Mactaggart & Mickel, and some time in the next few years Busby Road was realigned leaving the old line of the road as a lay-by (visible in the foreground of this picture). *Circa* 1970 the steep bank between Hill Crescent (background) and Busby Road collapsed, causing massive disruption and delay while the slope was repaired and reinforced. A footbridge once connected the garden of Busby House (now the site of River Court) with the Plantation area and until recently the holes for its supports could be seen in the wall of Busby Road approximately opposite where the gateposts to the old house stand.

The township of Sheddens grew up in the second half of the nineteenth century between Clarkston and Busby ('Sheddens' denotes a place where a main route splits into two branches). In *Busby and Its Neighbourhood*, William Ross mentions a Mr Gemmell's school here in 1880. The Craig family of Busby once lived here in Craigbank, a house with an adjoining grocer's shop. *Circa* 1926 the Sheddens Wine & Spirit Vaults became the Buck's Head Café.

Initially the builder of Holyrood Crescent had intended to construct tenements running right up to Busby viaduct, but his plans were halted when he ran out of money at the second close. As a result the name was later changed to Viaduct Road (the railway viaduct overlooks the tenements). One resident remembers engine drivers throwing coal to children playing near the viaduct, which was eagerly collected and taken home. According to Hugh Kelly, last manager of Busby gasworks, the tenement at the corner was built of recycled stone from the Upper Mill.

HOLYROOD CRESCENT, SHEDDENS, BUSBY.

The rear of Jackson's Court, possibly photographed in the 1930s when piping was being laid as part of the installation of inside toilets. All these properties, apart from one at the far end, have now been demolished and replaced by flats. The site is adjacent to the Sheddens roundabout where in 1902 the Sheddens Wine & Spirit Vaults stood.

The back of the Wakefield Terrace tenements at the Sheddens, photographed in 1938. These were built in the nineteenth century for mill workers. Two-storey blocks were also constructed in Burnside Terrace and Durham Terrace, while some cotton mill workers were housed at Smithy Row, situated where Lower Mill Road is today. Tenements and industry went hand-in-hand in Scotland during the industrial nineteenth century, and as the need for higher-density housing gradually became more pressing the old one-room cottages and two-storey cottage-type houses with outside stairs gave way to three- and four-storey tenements. The expansion of tenement-building was helped by the availability of good local quarry stone.

It was the arrival of the textile industry which led to Busby's growth. Cotton mill owners and calico printers had houses built for them in the form of terraces, usually referred to as lands (for example Carswell's Land). Stone tenements such as Craigielea (illustrated here) were also built during the 1880s and 90s. This was the period in which Busby's textile industry was declining and the village was becoming a desirable residential area from where people commuted to work in Glasgow. Craigielea stood on what is now the entrance to the car park behind the telephone exchange. This was built on the former gardens of Craigielea and Johnson's Land in Busby Road, opposite the Wakefield Terrace gardens.

Photographed in the 1950s, these four girls from Busby Laundry are, left to right, Ellen Lutz, Helen English, Peggie Dowie and Lizzy Brown. Busby Laundry was a major local employer from 1899 until after the Second World War. It was established by Isabella and Janet Alexander of Langside on nursery ground belonging to William McLaughlin and stood in Burnside Terrace, now Riverside Terrace, opposite two-storey terraces (later demolished) which housed mill workers. The laundry closed after a fire c.1965 and most of its buildings were demolished in 1968, although the large chimney wasn't removed until the 1970s. Local resident Bill Ferguson recalls men rushing onto the demolition site to get hold of the valuable lightning conductors from the chimney. The site remained vacant until the Riverside Gardens flats were built in the late 1980s.

James Denholm, driver of Busby Laundry's van, photographed with van boy Jimmy Brown. The picture is believed to have been taken in the 1920s. When James went to be interviewed by the Alexanders for the job of driver the firm was still using horse-drawn carts, but as a new and enthusiastic driver of three months' experience he managed to persuade Mr Alexander to invest in a motor van.

A more modern Busby Laundry van photographed c.1935, again with James Denholm as driver, this time assisted by van boy Donald Baillie.

Helen English, Lizzy Brown, Jessie Mitchel and Minnie Mitchel at work at one of the presses at Busby Laundry in the 1950s.

> Two women shaking and folding sheets
> What a wonderful sight from out in the street
> I remember the smell of boiling soap
> The strange metal machines that had to cope
> (From *The Busby Laundry* by Jean Fraser)

Blacksmith John Watt, in the centre of the picture, was the father-in-law of James Denholm (seen in the pictures on pages 21 and 22). John Watt plied his trade in the inter-war years when mechanisation was revolutionising agricultural life and the role of the horse was declining. During this period Busby's relatively rural surroundings were encroached upon as housebuilding continued, and farming lessened in importance as the number of commuters grew. At one time there were smiddys at Field Road in Busby; Waterfoot; Polloktown and Malletsheugh. This picture, dating from the 1920s, was taken at the smiddy in Ben View Road at Clarkston Toll behind what is now Houston's furniture shop. Before taking over the smiddy, Mr Watt had been employed with his brother at the Eglinton Arms, Eaglesham, looking after the horses stabled there.

This photograph shows members of Busby fire brigade, believed to have been a volunteer or wartime auxiliary brigade. The vehicle isn't a regular fire engine, and instead a private car is pulling a trailer pump. During the Second World War the local auxiliary fire station was located in the Arundel School at Clarkston. Fire stations were established in Paisley in the nineteenth century, Greenock in 1875, Pollokshaws in 1910 (transferred to Darnley in 1913) and in Johnstone c.1913. Busby's firemen originally belonged to East Renfrewshire Fire Brigade. When the Second World War broke out and the fire service was nationalised in August 1941, several brigades were joined as part of the Western No. 2 Area of the National Fire Service. In 1948 the fire service was denationalised and handed back to local authorities. Western No. 2 Area was broken up and Mr Bowman was then appointed firemaster of the Western Area Fire Brigade. This arrangement continued until May 1975 when Busby became part of Strathclyde Fire Brigade's 'C' Division with its fire station at Dorian Drive, Clarkston. The only individual who can be identified in this picture is Robert McFarlane, standing in the centre of the group at the front. The McFarlanes have a long association with Busby, and Robert and his family lived in East Kilbride Road and latterly Westerton Avenue. When Robert's father, Moses, died aged 82, his obituary appeared under the headline 'Passing of Oldest Native Resident'. He was described as 'one of the best known and esteemed personalities in our rural neighbourhood'.

This horse-drawn bus ran between Eaglesham, Sheddens and Clarkston where it met passengers from the Glasgow trains. The driver of the bus (with bowler hat and whip) is John Watt, the village blacksmith (seen on page 23), while the man standing on the right wearing the bowler hat is his father, Tam, who owned the Eglinton Arms in Eaglesham. Stables were situated behind the inn and milk carts would deliver milk from there to Glasgow. Anyone who was up early enough could get a lift back with one of these carts from Glasgow to Eaglesham. Tom Johnstone, who had a summer house in Eaglesham, often travelled back to Glasgow on the legendary horse-drawn 'soor milk cairt' which inspired him to write his well-known song of the same name: 'Whaur wi' the milk ilk morning, A little after three, We tak the road right merrily'. In the days of the horse-drawn bus Eaglesham was a holiday destination for Glaswegians who used the service to get to and from the village.

Busby railway station, built at what was the centre of the original village, was opened on 1 January 1866 to serve its expanding textile industry. Joseph Wakefield of Inglis & Wakefield, owners of the local printworks, was chairman of the Busby Railway Company which in 1868 extended the line to East Kilbride. A plan to continue the railway to Eaglesham did not come to fruition and the station which was to have been called Eaglesham Road became Thornton Hall in 1877 (it was renamed Thorntonhall in 1948). The start of the intended Eaglesham line can still be seen branching off to the right a quarter of a mile above Thorntonhall station where it served a lime quarry. Services to Busby and East Kilbride operated from the Caledonian Railway's South Side station (at Gushetfaulds in the Gorbals) before the opening of Central station in 1879. The presence of the railway was an important factor in encouraging Glasgow merchants to move to Busby and commute to the city.

The up line from Busby to East Kilbride being relaid at Busby station on 21 September 1975. Under the Busby Railway Act (1863), the Busby Railway Company was authorised to extend its track a further four miles from Busby to East Kilbride, an extension which was completed on 1 September 1868. Sidings were constructed for Busby printworks, the Giffnock quarries, various coal mines and the Thorntonhall lime works.

Ballasting the up line at Busby, 2 May 1976. These slow-moving wagons are being used to feed ballast (the stones that the sleepers lie on) onto the trackbed. The bridges and trackbed from Pollokshaws to Busby were made wide enough for double tracks, but the line was initially single track only. It was doubled between Pollokshaws and Busby in 1881.

Standard class 4MT 2-6-4T No. 80009 arriving at Busby with the 5.08 p.m. St Enoch to East Kilbride service on 12 June 1964, approaching the lattice post of a semaphore signal. The building on the down platform was destroyed by fire later that year, the last steam train to East Kilbride ran on 15 April 1966, and the semaphore signals on the branch were replaced by colour lights on 24 February 1974. There was a move during the 1960s to close Busby station but local residents were successful in their fight to keep it open. The *Statistical Account* of 1962 notes that 'The Busby–Giffnock–Thornliebank and Cathcart–Whitecraigs–Uplawmoor lines carry mainly Glasgow suburban traffic'.

Busby Lower Mill was built in 1790 by James Doxon 300 metres downstream from the Upper Mill and sharing its lade. Ownership of these two mills passed through various hands, with one of the most famous proprietors being James Crum, a member of the well-known family of Thornliebank calico printers. He acquired it in 1843. From 1888 to 1942 the Lower Mill was home to the Busby Bleaching & Beetling Company. The original building was destroyed by fire in 1968 but industrial units were built on the site and now form part of a business complex. Also visible in the picture are Busby railway viaduct (still in use) and Busby gasworks, built *c*.1830 and now demolished.

Busby Lower Mill. It was through the prosperity of the mills that Busby village really grew. Prior to the eighteenth century there was some small-scale industry along the banks of the White Cart including waulk mills (places where cloth was washed and thickened), corn and meal mills. As early as the 1660s John Parker, a Covenanter, had a waulk mill near what later became the site of Busby viaduct. Parker was executed in 1666 following the battle of Rullion Green. Busby's proximity to the major industrial centre of Glasgow, with its extensive export trade, made the village a particularly good location for manufacturing.

James Doxon devised an ingenious system of dams, lades and tunnels which linked his two mills and powered their water wheels. The remains of the weir and sluice of Busby Upper Mill are in Busby Glen Park at the path beside the swings. The Upper Mill was built beside the highest waterfall on the River Cart, the water being supplied to the mill by a short lade from a dam 25 metres upstream from the falls. Local researcher Stuart Nisbet took this photograph of one of the tunnels, floating a camera along it on a small raft and thereby bringing to light a sight unseen for nearly 200 years.

The first *Statistical Account* for the Parish of Mearns reveals that 360 people were employed in Busby's mills as early as 1799, of whom over half were under the age of fifteen. It was a six day working week with only two days holiday per year (apart from Sundays). Spinning of raw cotton was originally carried out in both the Upper and Lower Mill. Later the Lower Mill was used for weaving and finishing. Productivity was dictated by the speed of the machines and serious accidents, such as the severing of limbs, were not unknown due to a lack of safety regulations. In order to prevent cotton threads snapping, the atmosphere was kept hot and moist, conditions which encouraged diseases such as bronchitis, pneumonia, silicosis and tuberculosis. This photograph shows workers at the Lower Mill.

A printworks with a bleachfield attached to it was established by a firm called Kessock's at Busby Old Field in 1796, near the site of what had previously been a meal mill. An interesting incident during the company's time as owners of the works involved the forgery of the exciseman's official stamp. However, Kessock's inventive talent did not go undetected long and the government enforced the closure of the works in 1803. Macgregor, calico printers, acquired them in the same year but they were taken over in 1829 by McKean & Peacock. In 1842 Inglis & Wakefield became owners. There had been significant developments in calico printing over the previous few decades, during which cumbersome printing blocks gave way to machine printing using engraved copper cylinders. Inglis & Wakefield were incorporated into the Calico Printers Association in 1900, and the Busby works closed in 1901 with the loss of about 500 jobs. Having lain derelict for many years, the site eventually became part of the White Cart industrial area. This picture shows railway sidings serving the printworks.

Busby District School opened in 1876 with a roll of 540 pupils drawn from the parishes of Mearns, Carmunnock and Cathcart. The *Glasgow Herald* of Monday 31 January 1876 reported that the school had 'an elegant and attractive appearance and internally . . . wears a light, cheery, comfortable air'. In 1900 it was destroyed by fire, as seen in this picture, reopening on 12 February 1904 as Busby Public School with a library gifted by Capt. James Stewart of Williamwood. At the time the word 'public' was used to denote a state school rather than a private school. By 1939 the school had infant, junior, senior and junior secondary departments. In 1962 it became Busby Primary School and the building is now 'B' listed.

The Busby District School football team had the honour of winning the Gilmour Shield during the 1928/29 season. Boys in the team came from Busby and Eaglesham. One member, William Malone, is missing from the picture. He was a message boy and could not get time off for the photograph.

Back row: William McLean, William Couper, Sam Wilson, _____
Middle row: Mr Barr, _____, Mr J. Rodgers (headmaster), Tom Marshall
Front row: George Frame, William Bryce, Joe Fraser, Alex Gemmell

This photograph was taken at Busby District School in 1933. The teacher, Miss Donaldson (on the left) used to walk to school from Carmunnock every day. Two classes were combined for the photograph. The 'new' houses of Hawthorn Road can be seen in the background.

Back row, left to right: John Potter, Farmer Steele's son (name unknown), Willie Hopkins, ___ Wilson (farmer's son), Alec Rennie, Andy Wells, Charlie Harrier, Billy Taylor

Fourth Row: Miss Donaldson, Herbert Fairbairn, Jim Bothwick, Hugh Hume, Jack Herd, ___ Wallace, Tom Carlin, ___ Cowan, Dan McLean

Third Row: Sarah Currie, Isabelle Robertson, _____, ___ McNeill, Margaret Denholm, Nessie Baird, _____, Nanette Hawthorn, Mae Holmes

Second Row: Annie Hamil, Mary Young, Agnes Ferguson, Elsie McMillen, Jean Pickles, Isa Hendry, _____, Betty Killin, Nessie Barker, Nora Mullen

Front Row: Davie Duff, George Robb, Annie Parkhill, Nan Baird, Ian McPhee, Davie Brown

"Peace Day" at Busby

This peace celebration following the end of the First World War took place in the park of Busby School, which is visible in the background. An early photograph of the Duff Hall shows a large gun situated outside as a memorial where the car park is today at the corner of Main Street and Riverside Terrace. This was later removed. During the Second World War, Jean Fraser recalls the school railings being taken down in an effort to gather iron for munitions, and the name 'Busby' being removed from road signs 'to confuse the enemy'. She also remembers being frightened by the sound of 'Big Bertha', an anti-aircraft gun positioned over Busby Glen.

BUSBY AND CLARKSTON GOLF COURSE

Busby & Clarkston Golf Club was founded in the late nineteenth century when Busby was becoming a community of well-to-do commuters. It was the first golf club in Mearns Parish and survived until the late 1920s when its ground was acquired by Renfrew County Council to build houses on in the area of Hawthorn Road, Ellisland Road and Oliphant Crescent. The clubhouse was still in existence in the early 1950s. As well as offering its residents social activities via a variety of clubs and societies, Busby had a thriving sporting scene with Overlee Cricket Club, Busby Bowling Club and Cartvale Football Club all active in the village.

On 24 January 1881 a meeting was held in Clarkston Tollhouse to consider the erection of a Church of Scotland church in Busby. The four ministers of the surrounding parishes of East Kilbride, Eastwood, Mearns and Carmunnock were present, along with 10 laymen. Ground for the church was gifted by Mr J. D. Hamilton of Greenbank and it was opened on 13 April 1884. The architects were McKissack & Rowan. Although the church is now considered to be in Clarkston, its original name was Greenbank Church, Busby, and it was the first Church of Scotland church to serve the village. The park in the foreground is now the site of Hawthorn Court sheltered housing complex.

A Sunday school outing from Busby West Church, 1937. The man holding the cap on the left is Willie McVicar, church officer. Margaret Denholm, the donor of the photograph, is marked with a cross and is standing just to the right of centre. Busby West Church was opened as a United Secession Church on 8 May 1836. The Secession Church was founded in Scotland in 1773 by Ebenezer Erskine as a protest against the practice of patronage in the Established Church. The foundation stone of Busby West Church was laid by Dr Ross, brother of Revd William Ross, author of *Busby and its Neighbourhood*. With the growth of its congregation a gallery was added at the back of the church in 1844 by James Crum, who owned the Upper and Lower Mills at the time.

The Busby Spitfires were a local amateur dramatic group which met in the hall of Busby East Church where this photograph was taken. The group raised money to help buy Spitfire aeroplanes during the Second World War and Spitfire Gala Days were held locally. A collection of pots and pans was organised as part of the government drive to collect iron and other metals, and many railings were removed from local buildings too. Busby East Church, at the corner of Carmunnock Road, was initially called Carmunnock Free Church and was renamed in 1929. After formally uniting with Busby West Church in 1990, the East Church was sold and converted into flats in 1992. The development is called The Auld Kirk.

Jean Fraser and Betty Macmillan were maids of honour at Busby Gala on 24 June 1952. The gala was initiated just after World War II as a celebration at the end of the war and stopped taking place in the early 1960s, although it was revived in 2000 and is now held biannually. A committee of local ladies originally ran it (one member of which was Councillor Mary Young) and the Girls' Club was involved as well. The dresses worn by the queen and her maids at the early Busby Galas were usually borrowed and might have been bridesmaids' dresses, for example. Today dresses are purchased by the gala committee. Originally the Gala Queen and maids were chosen by voting which took place at Busby School, but more recently girls who wish to take part have been chosen by having their names drawn from a hat.

Dorothy Dowie is a maid and Ted Fraser a herald in this Busby Gala photograph, which was taken in the 1950s when boys also took part in the ceremonies. The children are probably standing on the lorry belonging to David Carslaw, the local coal merchant. The Carslaws had a number of businesses in Busby and were very involved in the local community. The Gala Parade used to start in the park on East Kilbride Road, then went along the Main Street to Busby School field where there was a stage. If it was wet the school or Girls' Club hall was used instead.

Joe Fraser, champion, and Robert Parkhill, herald, photographed with two members of the Braemar Ladies' Pipe Band in the Busby School field in the 1950s. The headmaster's house is in the background. A guest band usually led the gala parade up Main Street.

Oh! What excitement when came the big day
Of the Busby Gala, Hurray, Hurray
The sun shone bright, oh what a sight
Carslaw's coal lorry with flowers and bunting
Everything pretty nothing was wanting
Throne for the queen and seats for the maids
The centre piece for the big parade
(*Busby Gala*, 1953, Jean Fraser)

In the summer months during the late 1940s and 50s nearly everyone in Busby went to Busby Dam (on the river near Waterfoot) during warm weather. It was a very popular picnic area where bonfires were lit at night and sausages cooked on sticks. People still bathe in parts of the River Cart at Busby, especially at Busby Glen where a park was established in 1906 on land donated by local landowner Durham Kippen. There is a favourite spot in Busby Glen which locals call 'sandy beaches'.

A glorious day at Busby Dam *c.*1956. These bathing beauties would also have enjoyed the walks in Busby Glen Park, a haven for plants and wildlife which stretches as far as the Kittoch Water. A deep pool (above Busby Dam) known as Anderson's Hole, situated where the White Cart flows round the former garden of Busby House (now Bankholm Place), was another local swimming place. David Anderson recalls that 'Later when the "Golf Course" houses were built the local youngsters would use this same pool for swimming and fishing'. The swimmers pictured here are:

Back row: Jean Fraser, Irene Frame, Yvonne Lawson, Margaret Harris

Front row: Sheila Greer, Vera Hume, Senga Greer, Margaret Gorman, Anne Irvine

MOORE CONVALESCENT HOME FOR NURSES, BUSBY, GLASGOW.

The building that became Dr Moore's Convalescent Home for Nurses was originally one of two residences known as Busby House. It was turned into a convalescent home *c.*1897 when Dr Moore acquired it from its previous owner, William J. McKenna. The nurses used to use a bridge which once stretched across the road and gave access to Greenbank Church. In the 1960s the River Court flats were built on the site of the house and only its gateposts remain today, built into the boundary wall of the flats on Busby Road. Between these flats and the neighbouring tenements was St James Place which led via a steep, winding road down to Busby Old or Upper Mill.

Nurses Home, Busby.

The house eventually bought by Dr Moore was built in 1799 and seems to have been sold or rented to managers of Busby's cotton mills. One of the mills' owners, Mr Kelly, gave Busby House over for use as a hospital during the Asiatic cholera outbreak of 1832. In 1843 the mills passed to James Crum, a member of the calico printing family of Thornliebank. He greatly enlarged the property, building another house in the grounds as well as two lodges.

What is now the part of Busby on the west bank of the White Cart Water was originally a small settlement known as Newmill. Records of the ancient meal mill at the waterfall can be traced back to before 1300. Traditionally crossings were made between Busby and Newmill by fords above the waterfall and at Busby meal mill. In the 1780s the fords were replaced by a bridge as part of the new Paisley to East Kilbride road. According to a map of 1787 Busby originally consisted of only five houses on the Lanarkshire side of the Cart, two of them at the end of the bridge. The present bridge dates from 1939 and this picture shows it under construction.

The following extract from Stuart Nisbet's article, Crossing the White Cart, gives some background information into river crossings in and around Busby: 'Eastwood is bounded towards the north and east by the White Cart Water. In the early days roads were poor and bridges few and far between. Two hundred years ago fords were more common than bridges. Up to the end of the seventeenth century there was only one bridge over the Cart between Pollokshaws and Eaglesham. By contrast there were at least ten established fords on this stretch of the river, some having a particular use, such as Newford ford at Bonnyton which was a crossing point for lime for Eastwood farmers, from the workings at Thorntonhall. The earliest bridges over the Cart, near Busby, were at Pollokshaws, Cathcart and Kirklands (near Eaglesham). Three further bridges were added from the 1650s. A bridge was built at Dripps (Waterfoot) in the late seventeenth century serving the branch road to Kilbride. Busby bridge dates from

around the 1780s when it was built to link the two halves of the village and to serve the new road to Kilbride. From the 1750s major improvements were made to the roads in the area. The first completely new route through Eastwood was the Paisley to East Kilbride road commenced in the late 1780s. The following advert appeared in the Glasgow press at the time: "Notice to contractors for making Roads on the intended line of road between Paisley and Kilbryde. The Trustees are ready to contract with workmen for making the divisions from Peel Park to Busby Bridge and Busby Bridge to the Kilmarnock Turnpike (Eastwood Toll). Also for repairs to Busby Bridge, Spiers Bridge and Darnley Bridge and for building a new bridge near Mains of Eastwood." This new road through Busby superseded the traditional route to Kilbride via Waterfoot and Dripps. The old route remains today as a farm access road and is a good example of the poor alignment and gradient of a pre-improvement main road. Other new bridges soon followed. A second bridge at Busby served the expanding printworks. Bridges became a challenge to the traditional fords and ultimately led to their demise. The Trustees were losing valuable revenue as travellers were avoiding the tolls by taking the old ford routes and they sought to close the old routes. In 1794 the Trustees of the Turnpike Roads in Renfrewshire met to shut up several roads around Cathcart. Several roads in the Busby area were forcibly closed in 1797. With the abolition of the tolls in the next century, the good roads were free to everyone, and bridges were soon taken for granted.'

Bonnyton cottages, with the house on the left featuring the crow-stepped gables so often seen in Scottish domestic architecture of the seventeenth and eighteenth centuries. Revd Charles Miller of Dunse, who was born in Thornliebank, wrote poetry about Busby which included mention of Bonnyon, an area known as a local beauty spot:

> O Cartha! Fancy snatches me away
> To hear thy murmurs now by Finlay's mill
> And now by Bonnyton's romantic brae;
> Anon by busy hive of toil and skill;
> Then where the village bridge o'erspans thy pilgrim rill.

A song which mentions Bonnyton (also known locally as Bonnington), *Annie O' The Lee*, was set to music by William Moodie, a worker in the printfield, about 1870 and published by Swan & Pentland, Glasgow. Bonnyton Moor Golf Club was established as a public course *c.*1921 and was bought by the Jewish community after the Second World War when many private clubs didn't admit Jewish members. The Bonnyton Moor Golf Club exercised no restrictions.